Swing Trading Made Simple

Author: Mich

Translated fr(haus

Origir
Tradir ...crrugen Swing.

For questions and comments, feel free to contact the author: m.peroutka@gmx.net

All rights reserved. This book may not be reproduced in any form, in whole or in part, without written permission from the author.

Author's note:
The texts and contents of this book have been written with utmost care. I use the strategies outlined in this book myself. Please be aware, however, that the information contained in this book does not constitute a guarantee or promise of any sort, nor can the author be held liable for any losses resulting from using the information contained in the book. The mere fact that certain financial products are explicitly mentioned in the book does not imply that the author recommends purchasing, selling or holding these products. Stock market transactions entail risks that you should be aware of. When in doubt, you should always consult a professional investment adviser. Please be advised that the past performance of a security is not an indicator of its performance and profitability in the future. Any reader taking investment decisions and carrying out transactions based on the information in this book does so at his/her own risk!

Let me point out that trading in futures contracts, warrants and derivates (Contracts for Difference – CFD) comes with particularly high risks and may not even be permitted in your jurisdiction. Financial futures transactions may be highly profitable if you're lucky – however, they may result in great losses up to a point where you lose not only the amount you had originally invested but also extra money on top of that. Therefore, these transactions require in-depth knowledge of the financial products, the stock market as well as of different stock trading techniques and strategies.

Contents

Introduction

The Basics
   Money Management
   Trends
   Candlestick Charts
   The RSI Indicator
   The Slow Stochastics Indicator

The RSI-3 Strategy
   Setting the Indicators
   Example 1, Long
   Example 2, Long
   Example 3, Short
   Example 4, Short

Some Advice

Research and Time

A Few More Things

Introduction

In literature on finance and trading, you will find all sorts of share and forex investment strategies, many of which leave a lot to be desired in terms of clarity and guidance. The authors don't want to be held responsible for something they have written and don't want their strategy to be entirely transparent. Personally, I like to refer to this as the "gray area" in the books. In an attempt not to give away too much, the experts use vague terms such as "mental toughness", "the right instinct", "the hang of things" – concepts that are hardly understandable to amateur traders, especially when faced with the ever-difficult investor's dilemma: to buy or not to buy? When reading these things, I can't help but wonder why the authors (so-called experts or market gurus), who are obviously unwilling to completely disclose their successful strategy, publish a book in the first place.

True to the slogan "size doesn't matter", this book presents you with a detailed and targeted day-to-day strategy that allows you to specifically speculate on rising and falling share prices or exchange rates. You won't even require a sophisticated trading application: Trading at a day-to-day basis, you can maintain a relaxed attitude and approach to things without having to check share prices every hour.

The RSI-3 strategy is for those who see trading as a hobby and/or for investors who have little time on their hands due to other obligations like work and family. It is also a good strategy for people who are tired of day trading and the high risk that comes with it.

The advantages of the approach: a tight stop loss plus the fact that if the price moves in the right direction, the trade can be set to entry price at an early point.

But let's have a look at the basics first.

The Basics

Money Management

How much can you risk per position? Most investors tend to give little thought to this question. I know what kind of a challenge it is to engage in trading if you have little to invest in the first place. The lower the resources, the greater the tendency to take higher risks. In a decent money management strategy, these two things (generally) just don't go hand in hand.

There are solutions of course. However, the prospective profits will be lower, just like your account balance. As you know, low investment capital means that you can't buy too many shares. Let's have a look at the following table:

Trading risk

Balance	Risk (per trade)			
	2%	3%	5%	10%
$1,500	$ 30	$ 45	$ 75	$ 150
$2,000	$ 40	$ 60	$ 100	$ 200
$3,000	$ 60	$ 90	$ 150	$ 300
$5,000	$ 100	$ 150	$ 250	$ 500
$10,000	$ 200	$ 300		

The number of shares depends on the amount you can or want to risk (per trade).

Formula (long trade):
Shares = max. loss / (entry price − stop loss)

max. loss $60 / ($25 - $24.50) = 120 shares

Formula (short trade):
Shares = max. loss / (stop loss − entry price)

max. loss $60 / ($25.50 - $25) = 120 shares

For forex trades, you can calculate your risk as follows:

Value per pip =
(lot size * 0.0001) / exchange rate

AUS/USD
Value per pip =
(10000 * 0.0001) / 1.2400 = $0.81
(100000 * 0.0001) / 1.2400 = $8.06

EUR/USD
(10000 * 0.0001) / 1.3750 = €0.73

Don't forget to adapt the lot size. You can now use the value of $0.81 to calculate the best stop-loss level. For a lot size of $100,000 the stop-loss level is $8.06 (per pip).

If you persistently use trading risk tables and your (successful) set-up, you will certainly be able to enjoy your hobby for a long time to come while making a fair amount of extra cash.

Market Trends

How do stock prices change? They are controlled by offer and demand – nothing new about that. As long as investors are willing to pay higher prices, the share price will continue to go up. When nobody is willing to pay high prices, more and more shareholders will start selling their shares (to pocket the profits or maybe because of bad business news), resulting in falling share prices. Then, at some point, people will be tempted by low prices and start buying again. This phenomenon gives rise to trends!

Here's an example:

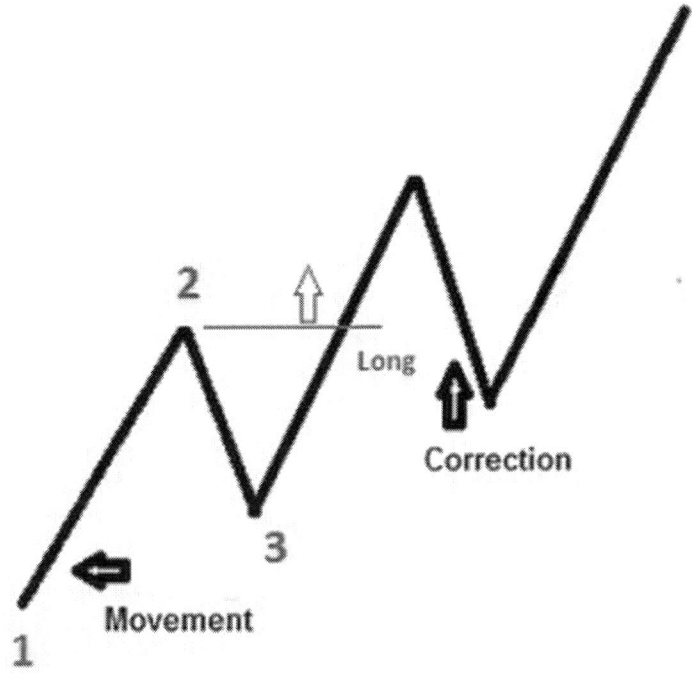

Figure 1, Upward Trend

Let's say you bought a share at point 1. While you are happy to see movement, i.e. rising prices and nice profits, other investors will also notice that the security is performing well and, wanting a piece of the pie, inevitably jump on the bandwagon. Once the share price reaches point 2, you decide to pocket the profits. After three consecutive weeks of rising prices, other investors follow suit. As a result, the number of sellers is greater than the number of buyers – nobody is interested in buying at prices that high.

The price correction takes place. With the entry price dropping again, people start changing their minds and buying new shares at point 3. The game has started again.

The downward trend can be described along the same lines, the difference being that the plus and minus signs change places.

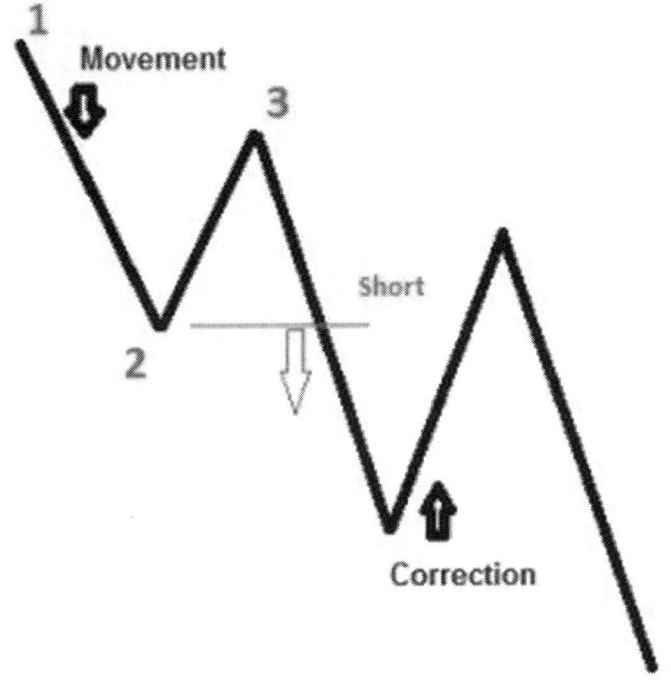

Figure 2, Downward Trend

For some reason (e.g. negative prospects for the company in question), more and more shareholders would like to sell their stocks. Point 1: the share price takes a dive. Stock funds may start flooding the market. At point 2, many people feel that the share is good value for money and start buying. Finally, point 3 sees different stake- and shareholder groups trying to sell their shares for different reasons (i.e. buyers from point 2 pocketing their profits, buyers from point 1 trying

to limit their losses, and funds selling at better prices compared to point 2).
All this fuss about the price is called a trend – a downward trend.

Examples of Trends

With a bit of practice, you should be able to identify the trend of a given share. Let's have a look at an example of rising share prices (upward trend).

First, without trend lines:

Figure 2, Henkel Share: Trend

Now, with trend lines:

Figure 2, Henkel Share: Trend with Trend Lines

These trends are actual trends and not textbook examples. I refrain from giving you such examples as they hardly reflect reality. The second trend is not perfectly neat either – but that's how things are in real life. Let's have a look at the Infineon share price:

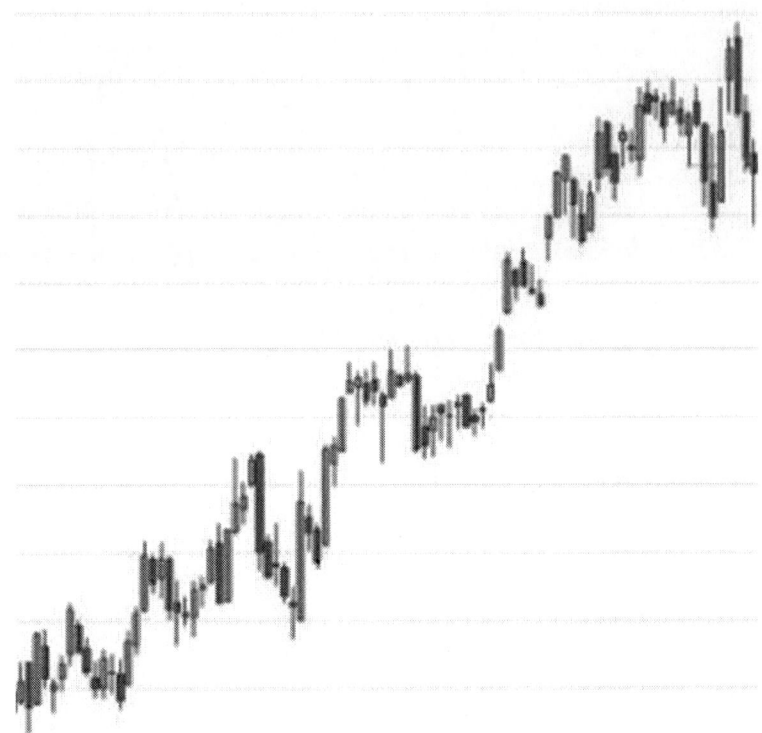

Figure 3, Infineon Share: Trend

And now with trend lines:

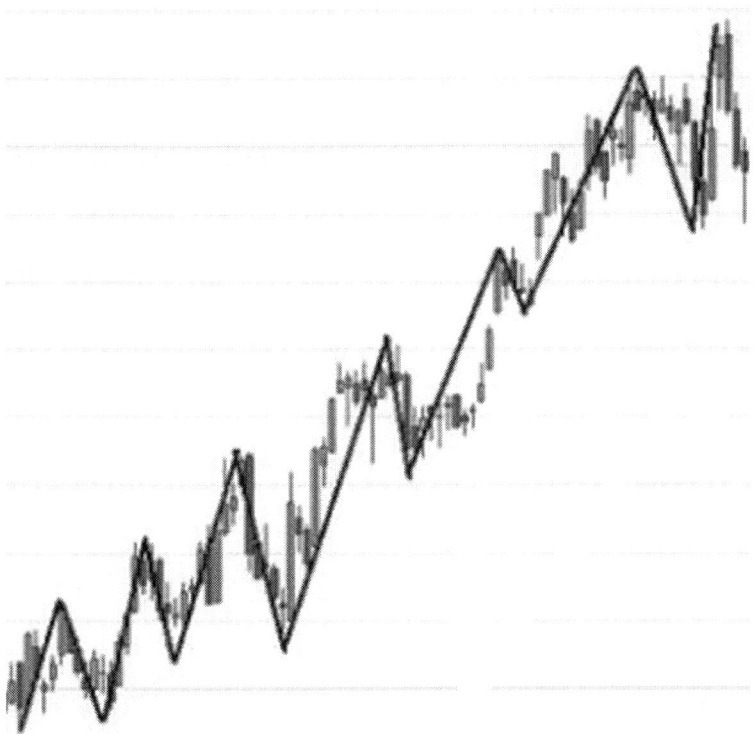

Figure 4, Infineon Share: Trend with Lines

To be able to speak of an upward trend, each successive peak and trough should be higher than the previous ones, even if it's only a few points or cents. The duration of the movement (also called progression) and correction (also referred to as regression) periods may vary.

These trends can also be found in indexes, e.g. the Dow Jones or Germany's DAX, as well as in exchange rates or any other underlying you would like to trade.
Now, let's have a look at a downward trend.

Figure 5, DAX Trend

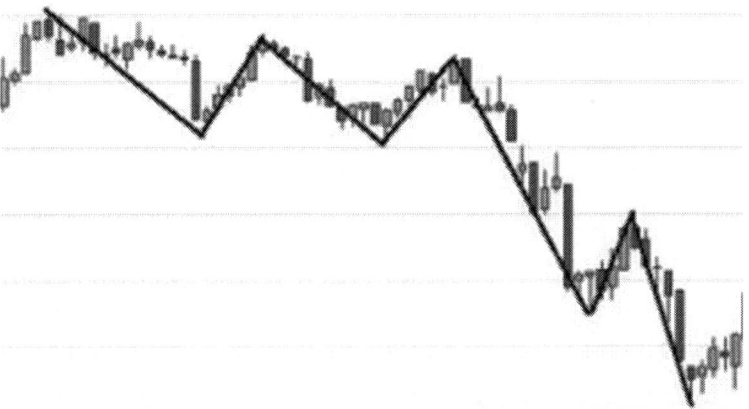

Figure 6, DAX Trend with Lines

Initially, the downward trend was not too bad, but then the index proceeded to take a steep dive.

Example 4 shows an upward trend in the Dow.

Figure 7, Dow Trend

And now with trend lines:

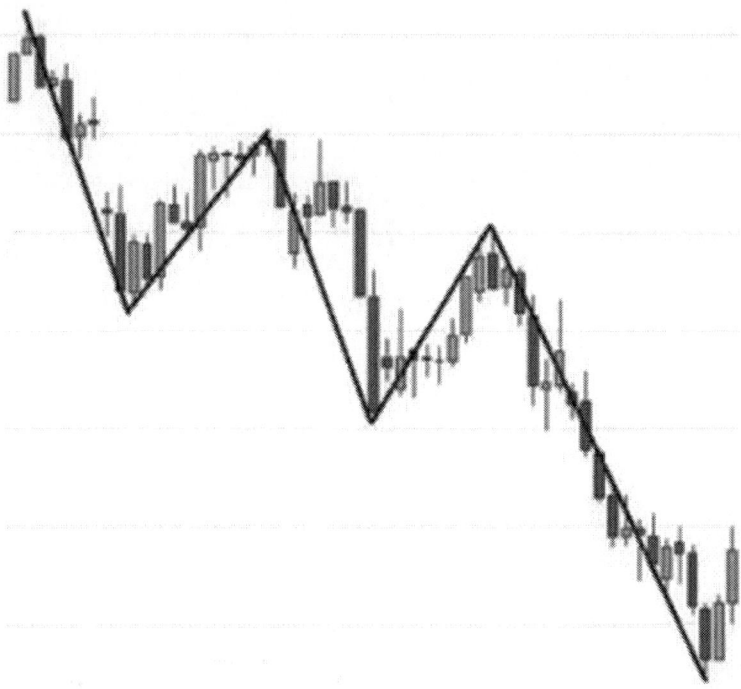

Figure 8, Dow Trend with Lines

A downward trend is characterized by successively lower peaks and troughs, as seen in the examples above (DAX and Dow).

Last but not least, there also is a third trend or phase. Markets and prices do not necessarily go up or down. When prices oscillate between a certain range with no distinct up- or downward movement, we speak of a sideway or horizontal trend.

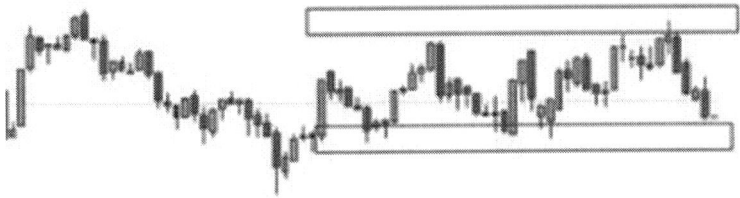

Figure 9, Sideways (Horizontal) Trend

During these periods, many investors may suffer losses because they tend to trade in the wrong direction and/or to misinterpret market signals.

Candlestick charts

In many charts, you can use "candles" instead of lines or bars. You may have seen such charts in other books. In most cases, authors and investors prefer candlestick charts. Each candlestick depicts the prices within a set time frame, i.e. five minutes in a five-minute chart or an entire day in a daily chart. Probably you're not too familiar with candlesticks: How to read them? What can they tell us?

Definition

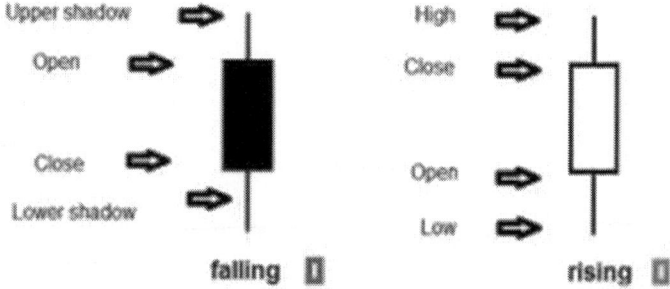

Figure 1, Candles (black: falling, white: rising)

The shape does not only tell us about the opening and closing prices: Individual candles or entire formations can mark turning points, i.e. bullish (rising prices) or bearish (falling prices).

Important Patterns

Let's have a look at some candlestick patterns:

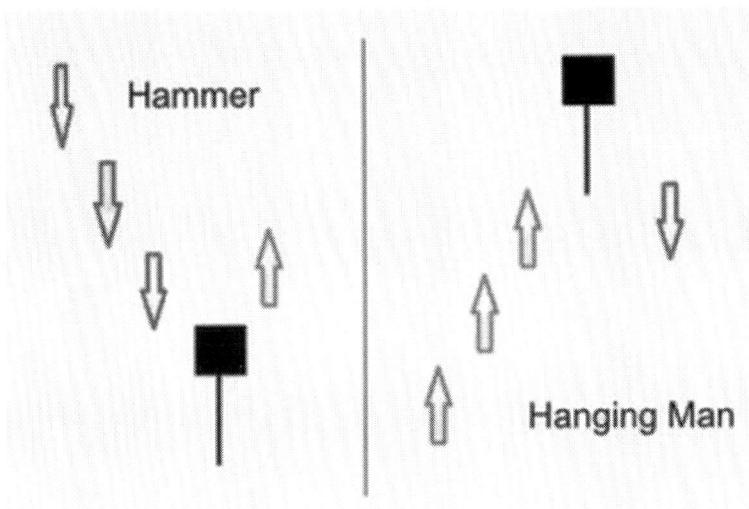

Figure 2, Hammer and Hanging Man

The hammer and hanging man patterns signal a turning point (that's why they are also referred to as reversal patterns!). The color doesn't matter in this case.

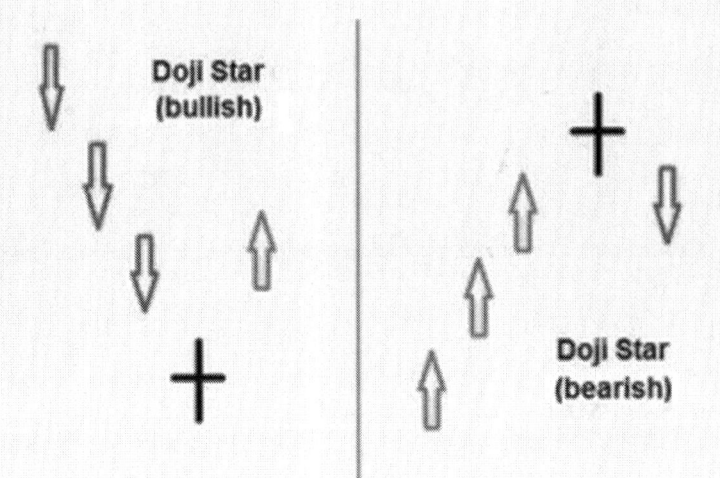
Figure 3, Doji Star

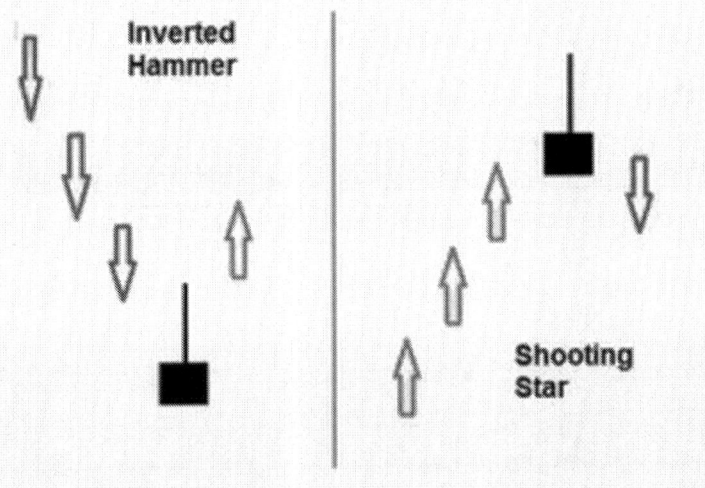
Figure 4, Inverted Hammer and Shooting Star

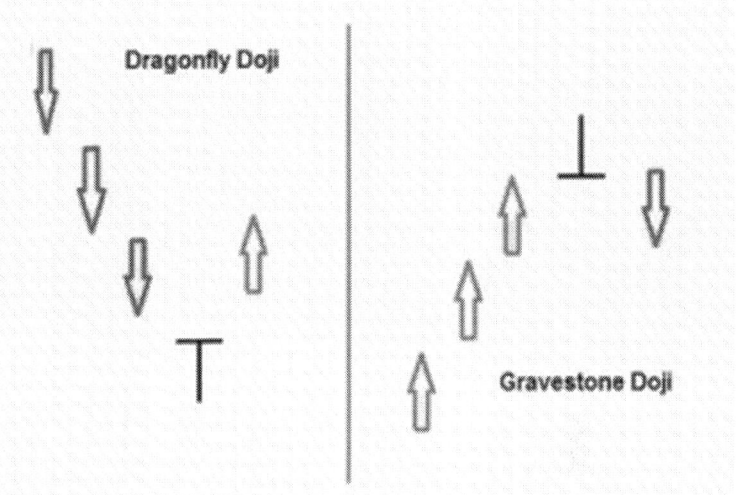

Figure 5, Dragonfly Doji and Gravestone Doji

Although these candlesticks are highly relevant, you shouldn't start trading like crazy or risk high amounts. Beware: There may be candles within a movement that do not signal a reversal of the current trend.

It is not until the end of a movement or a correction that you should pay closer attention to these signals. This is when you need to be able to interpret these signals correctly.

Examples (Candlesticks)

Figure 6, Trend with Candlesticks

Figure 7, Candles in a Trend

For an in-depth analysis of candlesticks, I recommended Steve Nison's book "Japanese Candlestick Charting Techniques", which contains detailed descriptions and examples of all the candlesticks patterns and their significance.

Summary

By know, you should be able to identify a trend and have familiarized yourself with important (reversal) candlestick patterns such as the „hammer". You should be able to mark them in a chart.

RSI - Relative Strength Index

The RSI (Relative Strength Index) measures the speed and change of price movements within a range from 0 to 100. Based on the past x periods (with the default being x=14), a security is considered to be oversold if the value is low; if the value is high, the security is considered to be overbought. The default ranges are defined as follows:

< = 30   = oversold;
> = 70   = overbought.

The default number of past periods (time units) is 14. You should check the RSI settings of your trading software.

For the scope of our strategy, we are going to set the RSI to three periods. This may differ considerably from the default setting, but it's vital for our approach.

Stochastics (Slow Stochastics)

Introduced by George C. Lane, the term "stochastics" may be ever so slightly misleading in this context as it has nothing to do with stochastics or statistical analyses. The misleading name notwithstanding, the term has become widespread, with many trading strategies being based on it. If used correctly – i.e. not as the only basis! – this approach can be very useful. The underlying idea is that during an upward trend, the daily closing prices are closer to the daily high. During a downward trend, the daily closing prices are closer to the daily low. Thus, a trend reversal can be identified when the closing prices start moving in the opposite direction. Once the closing price is the same as the daily high or low, the trend is considered to be over – a clear indicator of a reversing trend. Now, for the scope of our strategy, we want to use the Slow Stochastic Indicator. Please look for it in your trading software or web application.

RSI-3 Strategy

Setting the Indicators

It's only natural that people want to buy shares at good prices. I would like to show you a set-up that I have been successfully using for many years. I have chosen the Deutsche Bank share as an example, but of course you can use it for any other share. For liquidity reasons, I only trade U.S. shares or shares listed in Germany's DAX or MDax.

Trading Set-Up:

RSI (3) 80/20
Stochastics (6,3,3) 70/30
Share prices set to daily

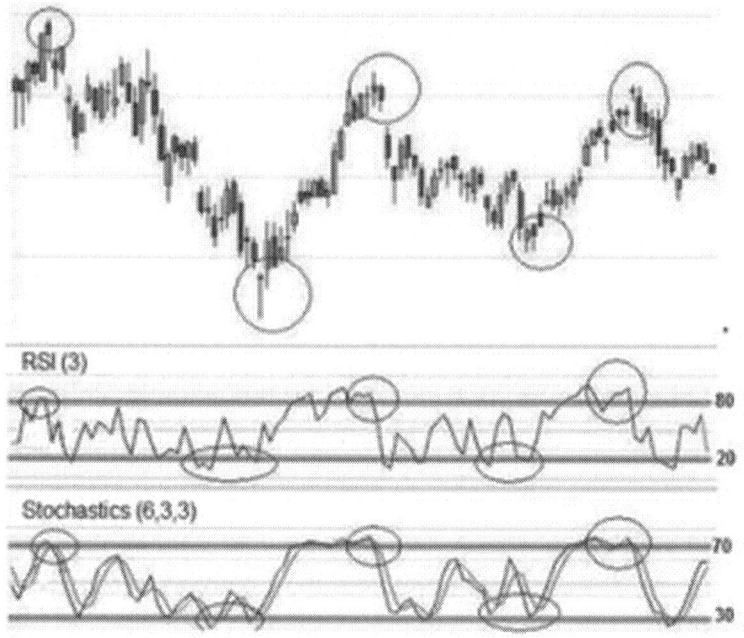

Deutsche Bank, Daily Prices, May-October 2013

Getting Started:

Find the Deutsche Bank share (or any other share that interests you). Set the chart to daily and the two indicators to the values above (RSI 3 and Slow Stochastics to 6,3,3).
Then, you can draw indicator lines at 80/20 for the RSI and 70/30 for the stochastics.

I have encircled the possible signals. Now you should be able to get a first impression of just how effective this strategy can be. We are focusing on the general assessment of the share here; hence, there is no need to display the share price at this point.

Normally, when trading a security, you want to start *with* the trend – not against it. Corrections can also be profitably traded. Another tool for the general trend direction is the Simple Moving Average (called MA or SMA; value: 200).

Example 1, Long

Having adjusted the chart settings, we are ready to start our first trade.

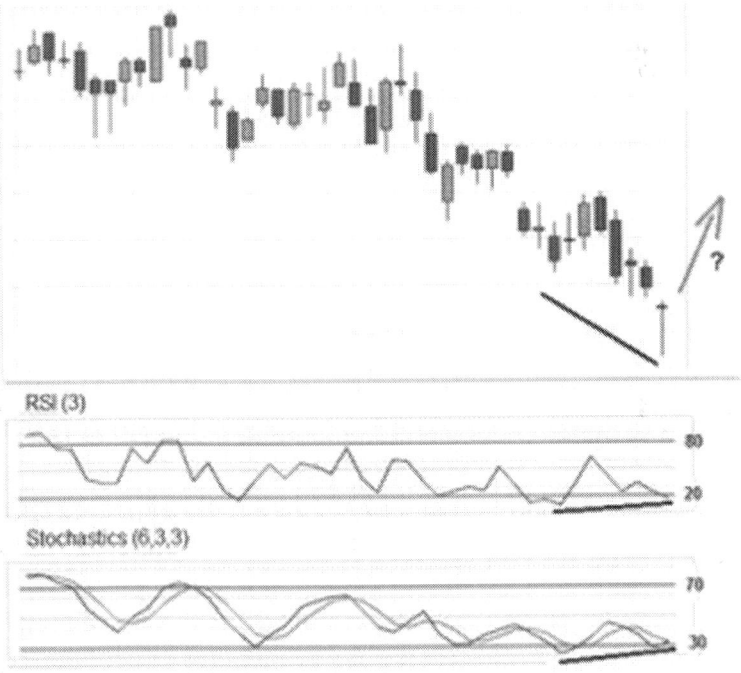

Deutsche Bank, Daily Chart

Looking for a good security to trade, the Deutsche Bank share can be identified as a reasonable choice. With the RSI below 20 and the stochastics below 30, i.e. near the minimum, and showing a divergence to the price, it is quite likely that the share price is going to see some movement (or a correction) within the next few days.

Thus, the trade meets several criteria:

- RSI and stochastics near the extremes
- Stochastics slightly increasing
- Divergence in the RSI (and stochastics)
- Relevant candle pattern for the day (Hammer/Doji)

We want to use the hammer or Dragonfly Doji (depending on definition, see basics) to start trading this position. We purchase at €31.70 and set the stop-loss at €30.40. Unfortunately, the stop-loss is far away from the entry price in this case, which has a considerable impact on the position size. When this is the case, I set the stop-loss at about two percent of the price, i.e. €31.05. This is a special case for long upper or lower shadows – quite reasonable to improve the risk-benefit ratio. For smaller candlesticks (and price differences), the default stop should be just below the upper or lower shadow.

The number of traded shares depends on your risk level (and bank account).

Risk Calculation (Example)

Formula:
Shares = max. loss / (entry price – stop loss)

Max. loss		
	Calculation	Number of shares
Risk in euros (or dollars)		
€ 50	50 / (31.7 - 31.05)	76
€ 100	100 / (31.7 - 31.05)	153
€ 150	150 / (31.7 - 31.05)	230
€ 200	200 / (31.7 - 31.05)	307

It doesn't make a difference whether the security you are looking at is traded in euros, dollars, pounds or any other currency – the approach is always the same.

Side Note: Common Calculation Errors

Note: Contracts for Difference are not permitted in some jurisdictions, such as the United States. However, this side note also applies to options and forex trades.

	Shares	Position	Margin (10%)
Capital			
€ 1500	76	€ 2400	€ 240
€ 1500	470	€ 14994	€ 1499

Traders, amateur traders in particular, often cannot resist the temptation of investing their entire available capital (e.g. €1500) with leverage (!), meaning that with a ten-percent margin, you would be able to trade some 470 shares per CFD. However, the risk that this entails is

€0.65*470 = €305, or about twenty percent of your capital. Is that so smart?

Let's say you are trading Deutsche Bank shares, and now you see an opportunity to purchase some Apple shares as well. But having no margin (or capital) left, you can't trade them. If you had used a different management, you would be able to trade these shares too, plus you'd be able to distribute the risk on several positions. It's important for traders to keep that in mind and to trade accordingly.

But back to our trade:

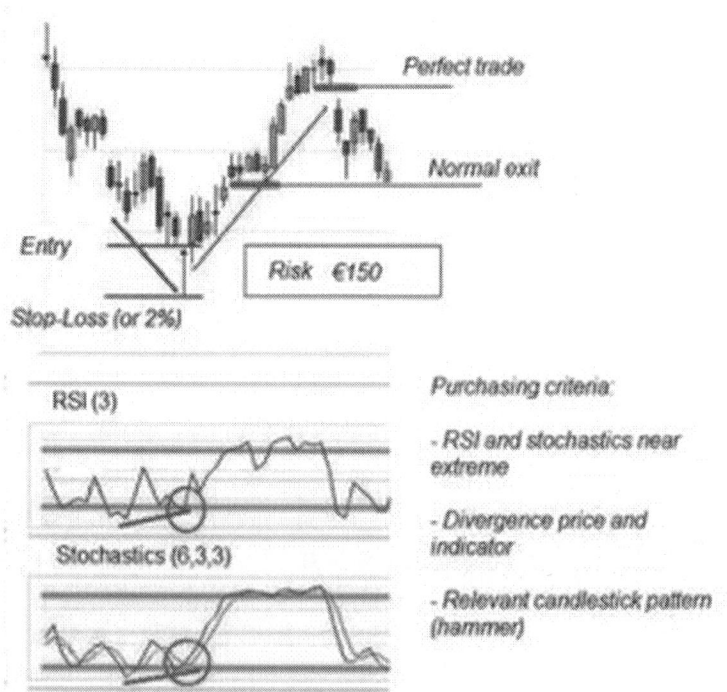

Deutsche Bank, Daily Prices

Our risk in this trade is 150 euros. That's (150 / (31.70 − 31.05) = 230 stocks (for the full stop/loss (150 / (31.7-30.4)) = only 115 Shares!).

Based on the daily candles, we adjust the stop every day, resulting in a stop price of about 33.20 euros on the sixth day, which is just a little below the sixth candle after purchasing. Unless a gap occurs the following day, our profit is (33.20-31.7)*230 = 345 euros. Now things are getting tricky. Many traders probably won't like the four-day sideways movement, meaning that most of them will decide to sell and pocket the profits at some point. That's not the end of the world though – our profits are more than twice the initial risk (risk at the beginning of the trade) of 150 euros. If you're of the adventurous kind, you could put some of your profits at stake (beware: a down-gap could mean that you'd be forced to sell at less than €33.20!), in which case you could sell for as much as €35.60 and make an impressive 897 euros. That would be the perfect trade. It's highly unlikely that anybody would last that long in reality though – most traders would probably sell at 33.20 euros and still make a decent profit.

What's the bottom line?

- The first signal: RSI and Stochastics near the extreme, preferably with divergence to indicators
- Purchase when a relevant candle pattern occurs, e.g. the hammer (or others)
- Adjust stop every day

Let's have a look at the possible profits (when selling at a realistic point).

A 1.50-euro profit per share when sold at €33.20.

	Profit (based on number of shares)			
Risk	76	153	230	307
€ 50	€ 114			
€ 100		€ 229		
€ 150			€ 345	
€ 200				€ 460

This trade is realistic even for a capital of as little as 1500 euros and a risk slightly above three percent (for CDF, options, certificates or other similar securities).
You will need more investment capital when buying normal shares. The profit is 114 euros or 7.6% of our capital – despite the fact that we chickened out even before the turning point.

Side note: Why not buy even earlier?

In this example, there was an opportunity to purchase a few days before (red circle). However, at least two of the necessary criteria had not been met: The divergence and, most importantly, the reversal pattern.

While the divergence may be dispensable, I would not buy unless there is a reversal candle. But in this case, there simply was not. Yes, you will miss out on some great opportunities and maybe you'll be angry. But let me ask you one thing: Why? Isn't it better to trade a set-up with the right criteria and to simply ignore these half-decent (but not decent!) opportunities? Let others take that risk! ;-)
You just lean back and wait for real opportunities and you'll see your hit ratio improve. Think about it.

Example 2, Long

The second example I prepared is a Daimler trade. Or maybe 'prepared' is not quite the right choice of words – I simply go through shares from the past two or three months (my old trades), trying to identify useful examples for you.

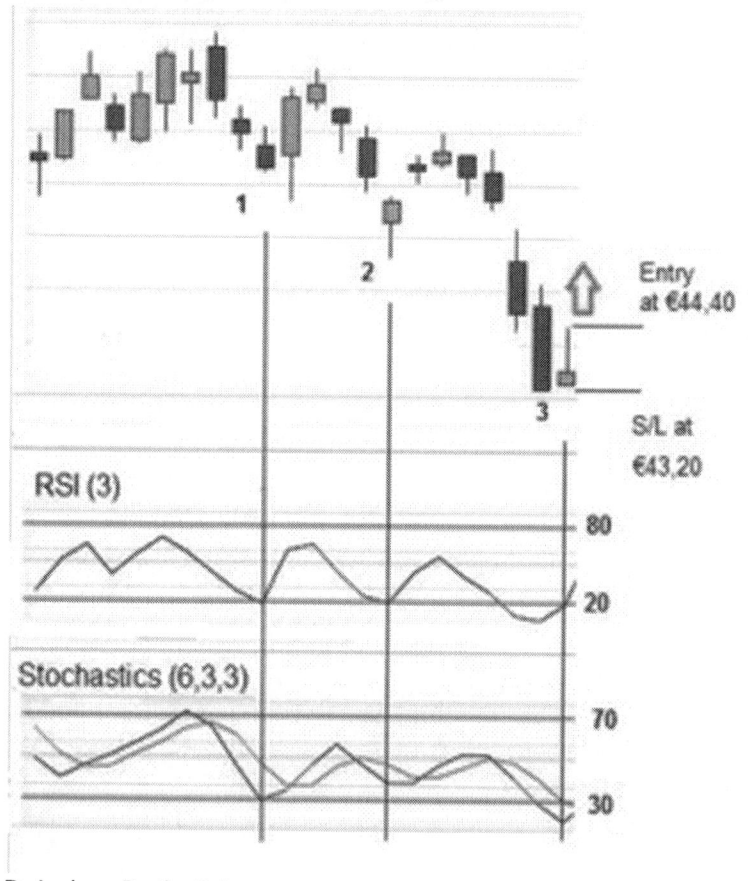

Daimler, Daily Prices

At points 1 (no real reversal pattern) and 2 (gap, the price practically has taken off), the conditions were not ideal. Things started to look better at point 3 though. The RSI and stochastics were considerably low, and the inverted hammer was clearly visible.

We decide to buy at €44.40, setting the stop loss at €43.20. Based on the difference and our initial risk, we can trade 125 shares.

Max. loss		
	Calculation	Number of shares
Risk in euros (or dollars)		
€ 50	50 / (44.4 - 43.2)	42
€ 100	100 / (44.4 - 43.2)	83
€ 150	150 / (44.4 - 43.2)	125
€ 200	200 / (44.4 - 43.2)	167

The following day, the share opens at €44.15. We're lucky that there's no up-gap, meaning that we can place our order. If the share price makes it above €44.40, we're in. Otherwise, the trade won't happen.

Let me show you what happened then:

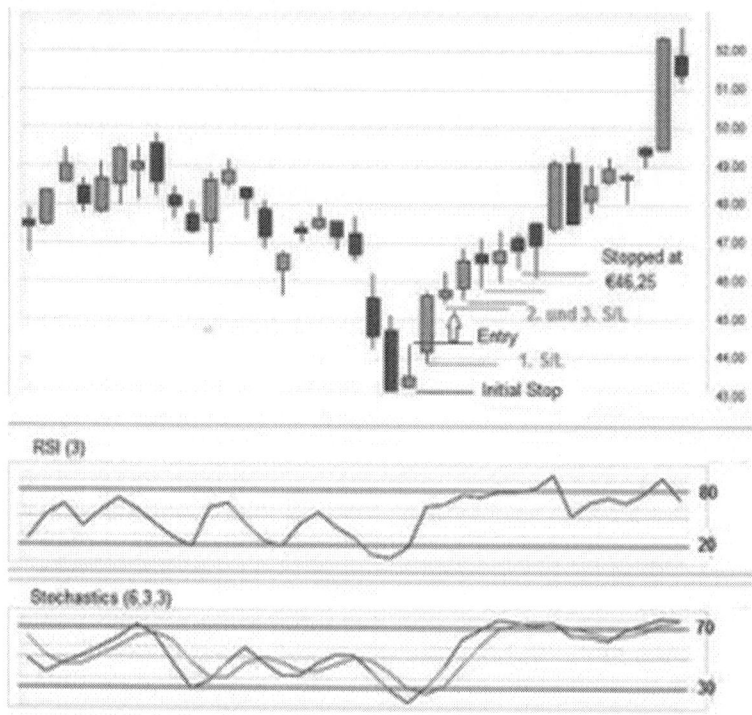

Daimler, Daily Price

We re-adjust the stop every day, setting it at a few cents below the daily low. Maybe this approach seems to be a bit boring – but that's all the "management" we need. There's nothing else to do, which saves us a lot of time!

After seven days, the position is stopped at €46.25. That's a €1.85 profit per share.

	Profit (based on number of shares)			
Risk	42	83	125	167
€ 50	€ 78			
€ 100		€ 154		
€ 150			€ 231	
€ 200				€ 309

Selling at this point is okay. Yes, it would have been possible to use a broader stop, meaning that we could have benefited from the rest of the movement and sold at €48.40. But that's nothing but speculation and wishful thinking. Let's look for other trading opportunities instead of crying over profits.

What's the lesson from this trade? Although we missed an opportunity when the gap occurred at point 2, we were able to trade the share a few days later. If we had jumped in at that point (point 2), we would have lost some of our capital. Once again, the criteria (this time, without the divergence) turned out to be the better approach.

Example 3, Short

Of course you can trade in the opposite direction, using similar criteria. The RSI and stochastics should be near the extremes. In this case, RSI >80 and stochastics >70.

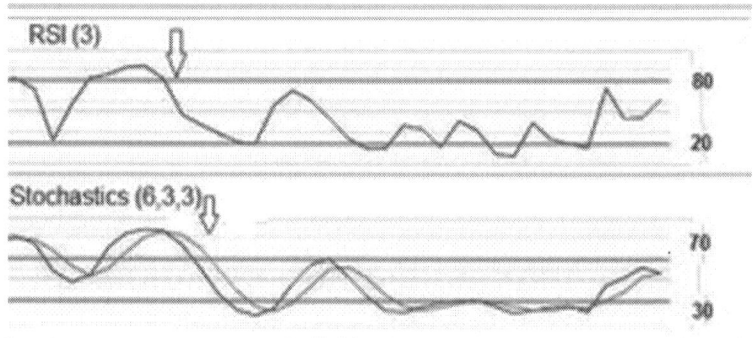

Caterpillar, Daily Price

Please have a closer look at this trade. Both indicators are near their upper extremes. The reversal pattern is very clear and no opening gap occurred. We can order at $89.50. We re-adjust the stops every evening for four days in a row. That's all there is to do. No trade management, no fussing around with the stop loss. The rules are clear right from the entry point.

Caterpillar, Daily Price

The second example also concerns the Caterpillar share. It's almost an exact copy of the first short trade. That's one characteristic of our strategy: it's easy to understand, the rules are clear and it can be copied over and over again. You can use this approach any time. If you lose something – which inevitably will happen sometimes – your savings never are at stake. On the contrary: In many cases, even a bad price development is stopped at break even. However, the few bad trades won't hurt the profits made from the good ones. You won't get rich overnight, but the earnings will be constant and you'll be able to relax (and you only need very little time).

Example 4, Short

Finally, I would like to show you a forex trade (euro/dollar). Of course you can trade any other liquid currency pair.

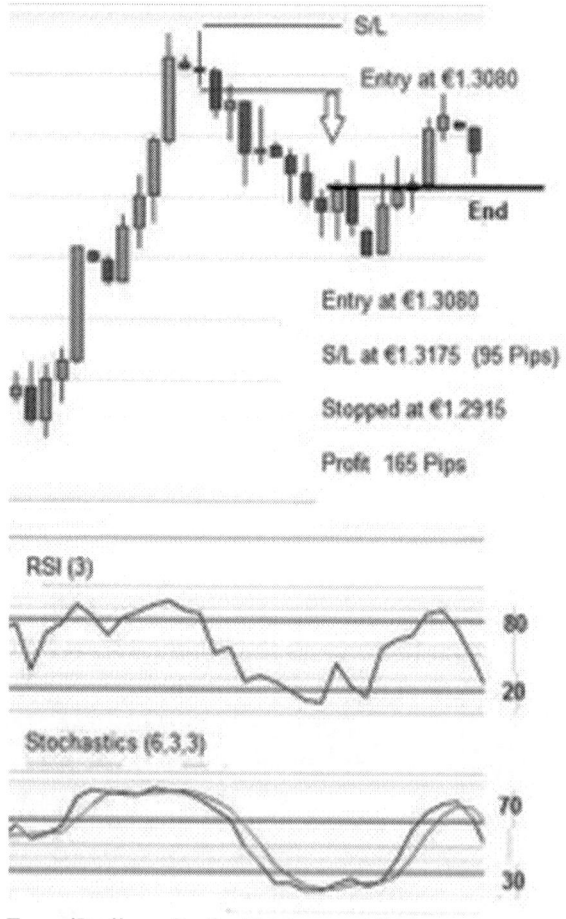

Euro/Dollar, Daily Exchange Rate

The approach is the same. Our starting position is slightly below the reversal pattern. We place a short order and we are stopped in. Please note that the stop loss of 95 pips is considerably higher than in normal intra-day trading. But remember: We're not using the one-minute or five-minute chart; we are trading at a day-to-day basis. This also means that the profits (number of pips) are considerably higher than in the shorter time frames. You should use the risk table and the number of pips to decide how much you want/can invest.

Here's the math again:

Value per pip =
(lot size * 0.0001) / exchange rate

Value per pip =
€10.000 euros * 0,0001 / 1,3080 = 0.76 euros

For 95 pips and 0.76 euros, the initial risk is 72 euros. The final profit is 125 euros.

Some Advice

Not all shares are suitable for trading. Some price developments clearly show why it's better to refrain from trying.

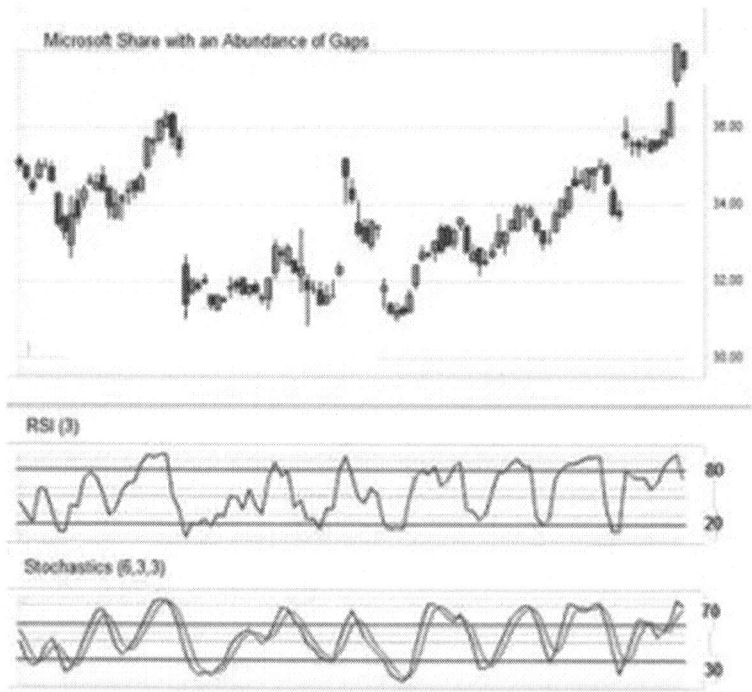

Microsoft, Daily Prices with Gaps

As a trader, you don't want to be at the mercy of those gaps. It's virtually impossible to assess the risk. And even if you're lucky once and the price moves in the right direction, you might be stopped with a much larger gap next time. You should trade other shares – there's more than plenty to choose from. Or wait at least until things have calmed down.

Research and Time Expenditure

In terms of time, you won't have to do a lot. You should look for interesting shares. In the morning, you should check what happens upon opening (gaps?) and place your order. In the evening, all you have to do is move the stop loss. To speed things up a bit, it makes sense to use automatic share screening. As far as I know, some brokers have scanners allowing you to filter shares according to your criteria (RSI and stochastics). Otherwise, you'll have to invest 15 or 20 minutes of your time every evening to scan the Dow. And that's all you should trade for a start. Once you get the hang of it, you can try foreign shares (e.g. listed in the DAX) or currencies. Depending on your time and priorities, you can only trade U.S. shares. Stick to liquid securities and a large market cap.

Final Notes

<EBook> Just a few more things: The layout and images have been adjusted for different reading devices (Kindle, Kindle Fire, Apple iPad). Unfortunately, the different display sizes of different e-readers may result in paragraphs or pages of a few lines only. My apologies for the inconvenience.

Any useful review on Amazon is greatly appreciated. Please don't compare the number of pages and the contents with the big textbooks out there. I don't when I determine the price. You get decent value for your money – if you use this book correctly, your first successful trade can be much more than some extra dough in your account. It could change your entire approach to trading.

Last but not least, I would like to recommend the following book:

"Die entspannende Jagd zum Erfolg" – Trading Strategies, Volume 1.

This book provides an overview of different trading set-ups, both for short trades based on the five- or ten-minute chart and for position trading over several days. Once again, the examples are realistic and comprehensible. Why not go to Amazon and have a look?

Currently only available in German. Watch Amazon.com for new titles in English by this author.

You'll find my e-mail in the imprint. I'm always open to questions and new ideas.

Enjoy your hobby, make some nice profits out there and take it easy!

Printed in Great Britain
by Amazon